Primary Hinduism

Seeta Lakhani

Edited by Jay Lakhani

	Hinduism for Schools site : http://www.hinduism.fsnet.co.uk
m	Schools must register with us to gain access to our constantly updated website offering activities tailored to Key stages 1/2/3 requirements: hindu@btinternet.com
e 4 +	Hinduism for Schools textbook by Seeta Lakhani ISBN 0-9549567-0-2
T	Click on Secondary & Primary School Resources links at http://www.hinduism.fsnet.co.uk

ACKNOWLEDGMENTS

The author and publisher thank the following for their contribution:
Most illustrations by: P. S. Babu
Front and Back Cover: Robert West

Note: The word 'man' in 'divinity of man' or 'HE' for 'God' has been used in this book in the most generic sense. This should not be seen as a bias in favour of the male gender.

ISBN 0-9549567-1-0

First published in 2006 by:-
Vivekananda Centre London Ltd
6 Lea Gardens Wembley Middlesex UK HA9 7SE

Designed and Printed in Singapore by Graphics Zone

Contents:

This book is dedicated to

Holy Mother Sri Sarada Devi

Author's Thanks

I am tremendously grateful to a number of people for their kind help and encouragement in writing this book. In particular, I would like to thank Prakashbhai and Raj for their invaluable suggestions on the artwork and layout of the book, and for giving so generously of their time. I am grateful to Elsie Mack for her thoroughness in proof reading and for giving the text greater clarity and comprehensibility. I am indebted to Dr. S. Budhdeo for subsidising this publication. Special thanks go to P. S. Babu for creating wonderful illustrations that fit so well with the narratives.

Most of all, thanks go to my father for his exceptional guidance in the presentation of elementary Hinduism in a simple and beautiful way, for his meticulous editing, and his infinite patience.

Seeta Lakhani

Teachers' guide notes:

This book has been specifically designed to address the requirements of teaching Hinduism at key stages one to three (for ages 5 to 14) in a format that is in line with the guidelines suggested in the new non-statutory framework for religious education. The task of producing a textbook that can engage pupils of such a wide age range has not been easy. We have tried to achieve this through greater usage of the narrative dimension of Hinduism. The narratives have been sensitively chosen not only to convey the key teachings of Hinduism but also to present them in a modern context.

At the end of each chapter we have offered a summary table that makes the distinction between learning *about* and learning *from* religion. In these tables we have also incorporated many ideas for classroom activities specially designed to help with the knowledge, skills and understanding criteria suited to religious studies.

We have developed some novel themes that draw on the breadth of vision of Hinduism. Ideas like religious pluralism, experiential religion, inter-faith dialogue and spiritual humanism come very naturally in Hindu teachings. Because of its pluralistic approach Hinduism has a great deal to contribute towards exploring variations within and between religions as well as variations between religious and non-religious world-views.

Discovering spirituality in a non-theistic mode or even in a non-religious mode through arts or sciences are areas we have touched upon in this textbook. This feature of Hinduism makes it very endearing to pupils and teachers with no religious affiliation. For continuity and coherence of teaching Hinduism at Key stages 4 and above consult our publication *Hinduism for Schools*.

Teachers can access further resources and ICT links by visiting our website Hinduism for Schools at http://www.hinduism.fsnet.co.uk . Pronunciations of the key Hindu terms can be accessed through our website. Teachers can register with us to get on-going support and constantly updated activities packs to help them with their teaching activities by emailing us at hindu@btinternet.com

This book draws on the experience of presenting Hindu teachings to thousands of pupils in hundreds of English schools.

Jay Lakhani (Editor)
Vivekananda Centre London

Chapter 1
What is Hinduism?

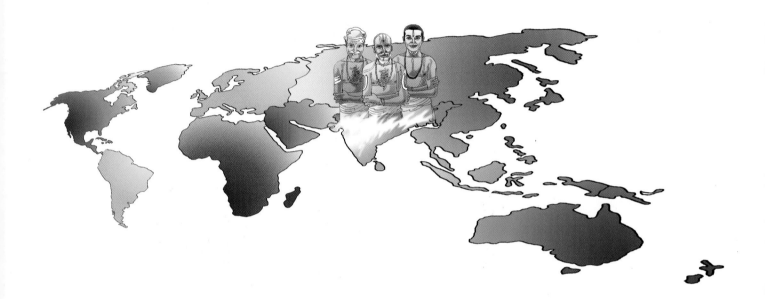

Hinduism is the name of a religion that began in ancient India thousands of years ago. Today there are nearly a billion people in the world who practise this religion. These people call themselves Hindus.

From Sindhu we got the word Hindu
The word Hindu comes from the name of an ancient river in India called the Sindhu. Some people could not pronounce the name of the river Sindhu properly. They pronounced it as Hindu. The people who lived in that part of the world then became known as Hindus.

Hindus call their religion Dharma

Dharma means trying to make sense of the world and our place in it. It teaches us to treat everyone and everything with respect. The way Hindus practise their dharma is by being good and doing good to others. Hindus are not only expected to look after their families, but also to look after everyone and everything. Dharma makes us think hard about what this world is all about and our role in it.

Rishis are the founders of Hindu religion

Since ancient times, there have been people who have been able to see or experience God for themselves. Hindus call these special people rishis. They can be men or women. They can be young or old. They may have lived a long time ago, or they may have lived in recent times. They are very special because they can teach us about God.

The story of a young girl called Vak who became a rishi

A long time ago, in ancient India, lived a little girl called Vak. She was a real chatterbox. She would just not stop talking. One day, Vak was trying to talk to her mummy who was very busy in the kitchen. Vak's mummy got a bit annoyed. She said, 'Vak can't you see I am busy? Be quiet!'

Vak went quietly up to her room and sat on her bed. She felt very sad and started to cry. She wiped away her tears and thought: 'I will now sit still and not talk for ever and ever.' She closed her eyes and sat still...she sat very still and was very quiet. Every time she wanted to speak or fidget she controlled herself and kept absolutely still. She sat still for hours. Even her thoughts became still. Only exceptional people can be still for such a long time. After some time, she saw a brilliant light. She could also hear a sound that seemed to come from everywhere and sounded like **Om**. She was experiencing God. This is called a spiritual experience. Sometimes when we see something awesome and beautiful, we gasp in delight. Spiritual experiences are a bit like that, except they are far more intense.

After some time, Vak opened her eyes. She had been still for hours! Vak had experienced God! She felt wonderful. Vak had now turned into a rishi. From that day on, Vak was very special. She could tell everyone about God. She was still a chatterbox, but now she chattered only about God. Everyone listened to her in amazement. What she said made a lot of sense. She became very famous in the whole country. She taught the people that it is not enough to believe in God; we must try and experience God for ourselves.

This story tells us that just like the little girl Vak, we must try and control our minds to get a spiritual experience. Some of us get a glimpse of what spiritual experiences are like when we see something awesome or beautiful.

Religious symbols are a way to think about and link with God

We use symbols to help us think about things. For example, we may use a logo for our school, or a flag for our country. In the same way, we also need symbols to help us think about and link with God. Two of the most important symbols Hindus use, are **Om** and the **Swastika**.

Om is the best name for God

All rishis who go into deep meditation and experience God, hear the sound Om. This is why the Om sound is very important for Hindus. They say that it is the best symbol or name for God. Hindus use the word Om at the start of their prayers and sometimes chant Om when they meditate.

Swastika means: 'Let good luck come to us from everywhere'

This symbol is meant to bring good luck. It has a shape that points in four directions. It means: Let auspiciousness or good luck come to us from all four corners of the world.

Lotus is a symbol of purity

Even though the lotus flower grows out of muddy water, it emerges pure, beautiful and detached. In the same way, Hindus are encouraged to lead pure lives.

Tilaks are Special Marks on the Forehead

Some Hindus put a mark on their forehead; this mark is called a tilak. Different Hindus may use different markings. Some put a round red dot on their foreheads. Some Hindus mark their foreheads with three horizontal lines. Some mark their foreheads with a U shape and a dot in the middle.

Hindu Teachers are called Gurus

Teachers who help Hindus learn about their religion are called gurus. They answer our questions about who God is, and how we may find God.

Holy people are called Swamis

Swamis are monks. Swamis wear orange clothes. They leave their homes and families and stay in monasteries. They wish to find God by helping others. One swami who became very famous and found God by serving others was Swami Vivekananda.

The best way to teach is by setting a good example

A young boy called Nilkanth joined a monastery, a place where holy people live and think about God. The boy worked hard and helped with all the daily jobs like washing clothes, collecting firewood from the forest, and cooking and serving food. Everyone was amazed to see how hard the boy worked. This boy set a wonderful example of how to serve others. He taught that the best way of teaching something is by setting a good example. Everyone liked this hard-working boy. He later became the head of the **Swaminarayan** movement.

This story tells us that the best way we can teach others is by setting a good example. Nilkanth worked hard to serve others and set a good example for others in the monastery to work hard and look after others.

Learning about Religion

- ❖ The word Hindu is derived from the name of the river Sindhu
- ❖ Dharma means 'making sense of the world and our place in it'
- ❖ Looking after everyone and everything is the way of putting dharma into practice
- ❖ A Rishi is a person who can see or experience God
- ❖ Om is the name of God heard in deep meditation
- ❖ Swastika means: Let good luck come to us from all the four corners of the world
- ❖ A Guru is a religious teacher
- ❖ A Swami is a monk who wishes to find God by serving others

Learning from Religion

- ❖ Religions are based on the spiritual experiences of some individuals
- ❖ Experiencing God for ourselves is the best way to know about God
- ❖ Can we be spiritual without being religious?
- ❖ Symbols give a sense of identity and belonging
- ❖ Religious symbols can be used to link with God
- ❖ We need symbols to get our minds around subtle ideas. We do this in mathematics (x, y, z in algebra or infinity in arithmetic)

Classroom Activities

- ❖ Name the prophets of other religions.
- ❖ Visit the Hinduism for Schools website and download symbols Om, Swastika and Lotus. Paint them using bright colours
- ❖ Hear how some of the Hindu words are pronounced by moving the mouse over the words at the bottom of the pages on this website
- ❖ Name the symbols of other religions and comment on their special features
- ❖ Make Tilaks on the forehead. Use only washable powder or paint. Dip the third finger (considered auspicious) in paint or powder to make the marks. Girls can wear detachable bindis as fashion accessories to go with different coloured clothes

- ❖ **Discuss:**
1. What would a spiritual experience be like?
2. What happens when we try and sit still to meditate?
3. Are spiritual experiences possible only through meditation?

Holly Cross
(Jesus Crise)

OM

Islamic
or
Islamic

Star of David

Victory

Dharma Chakra
(Buddisum)

Jainisim

State Religiean of Iran

Zorastrinianism (Forohan)

Judisium

Chapter 2
Thinking about God

Pluralism

Even though there can be only one God, different people think of God in different ways. Many Hindus like to think of God as a father in heaven. Some Hindus like to think of God as a mother in heaven. Hinduism says that there are hundreds of different ways to think about God. Some Hindus think of God as their best friend. There are some Hindus who even like to think of God as a little baby. The important thing to remember is that even though there is only one God, there are many ways to relate to Him. This is called **pluralism**. Hinduism teaches that different religions are different ways of thinking about the same God.

My mum is the best

There were two boys who were best friends. They liked to play football. One day while they were playing, one boy said, 'My mum is the best in the world.' The other boy disagreed. He said, 'My mum is the best in the world, she cooks the best food.' The first boy said, 'That is not true, remember you brought those home-made cakes last week, they were like rocks! Your mum is not the best in the world, mine is.' Now both the boys loved their mums very much and thought their mums were the best in the world, so they started to fight over it. Soon they were hitting each other and getting bruised. A wise man passed by and asked why they were fighting. When the boys explained the reason for their fight, the wise man suggested, 'Why don't you both say, 'My mum is best' but then add two magic words at the end of the sentence, then there will be no reason to fight each other. Say 'My mum is best *for me.*' Both the boys agreed that this is what they meant in the first place. Their mums were best for *them,* not for everyone else. They again became best friends and started to play football. This is what pluralism teaches: Each one of us can say my religion is best *for me,* but we must not say that it is best for everyone else too. Other people may have their own religion (or sometimes have no religion) and that is best for them.

Vivekananda brings the message of pluralism to America
A famous person called Swami Vivekananda brought the message of pluralism from India to the West about a hundred years ago. He taught that all religions are different ways of becoming spiritual. No one religion is better than another. The religion that suits our needs is the best for us. We must not fight that our religion is better than any other. He also said that there are many people who can be spiritual without believing in God. For example in the Buddhist and Jain religions there is no need to believe in a God. There are many other ways of becoming spiritual without having to believe in religion or God.

Thinking of God as a little boy ~ The Story of Gopal-Ma

About a hundred years ago in India, lived an old lady called Gopal-Ma. She liked to think of God as baby Krishna. She had a little statue of young Krishna. She prayed in front of the statue every day. She was not happy just seeing the statue of Krishna, she wanted to see the real Krishna. Many years went by.

…One day when she was praying, something very strange happened. There in front of her, was no more the statue of young Krishna, but the real boy Krishna, smiling and looking back at her! Krishna started to play with her, tugging her sari, and asking for sweets. She was amazed! She rubbed her eyes. She could not believe what she was seeing. But there in front of her, stood Krishna, being naughty and bothering her for sweets!

Gopal-Ma was so happy, tears of joy flowed from her eyes. She gave sweets to Krishna, and she talked and played with Him. Imagine what fun it would be to actually see God as a little child! Gopal-Ma spent the rest of her life thinking of God and loving God as Krishna. This is the true story of how someone was able to see and play with God in recent times.

The story tells us that if we truly love God and desire to see Him, he will come to us in the form we like. Gopal-Ma liked to think of God as young Krishna, so God appeared in front of her as young Krishna. God can be experienced in meditation; He can also be seen as a real person!

God as a father figure in Hinduism:
Brahma, Vishnu or Shiva (Three in one: Trimurti)

Brahma
When Hindus think of God as a person who is responsible for creating the universe, they call him Brahma. He is shown with four heads to see in every direction. He has four arms and holds holy books. He sits on a lotus flower.

Vishnu

When Hindus think of God as a person who looks after the world, they call him Vishnu. He has four arms. He holds divine weapons to destroy wicked people. When Vishnu is born on earth he is called an avatar. He comes to earth to teach people about religion and to protect good people. Two famous avatars of Vishnu are Rama and Krishna. Many Hindus worship Rama and Krishna as God.

Shiva

Some Hindus like to think of God as Shiva. They like to think of God as both the creator and destroyer of the universe. Shiva is shown sitting in meditation. The river Ganges streams out from his hair and a snake is seen curled around his neck.

God as a mother

There are some Hindus who do not like to think of God like a man. They prefer to think of God as a woman, so they worship God as the Mother Goddess. The Mother Goddess is the source of all power and strength. She is called **Shakti**, which means power. 'May the force be with you' actually means 'May the Mother Goddess help you.' God as a mother can be seen in many different forms.

Parvati and Durga

Parvati is one way to think of God as the Mother Goddess. Parvati is the source of all power, Shakti. When she wants to destroy wicked people, she changes herself into Durga. Durga is shown sitting on a tiger or a lion and holding many divine weapons to fight evil.

Saraswati

Another way to think of God as a mother, is Saraswati. She is the Mother Goddess who helps us become clever in art, science, music, and dance. She is shown wearing a white sari and holds holy books, and a musical instrument called the veena.

Lakshmi

Another way Hindus think about God as a mother is as Lakshmi. She is the Goddess of wealth and beauty. Lakshmi is shown wearing a red or pink sari, offering gold coins to her devotees. She is shown sitting or standing on a pink lotus flower.

Rama and Sita teach us how to lead a good life

Rama was born thousands of years ago as an avatar of Vishnu. Rama was honest, upright and perfect in every way. He lived a noble life helping others. Sita, his wife, was loyal, kind and gentle. Every Hindu girl tries to be like Sita. Rama is shown holding a bow. He is accompanied by his wife Sita and his great friend the brave monkey God, Hanuman. The Ramayana is a holy book of the Hindus. It narrates the adventures of Rama, Sita, and Hanuman. Hindu children learn about their religion by reading stories from the Ramayana and by following the example set by Rama, Sita and Hanuman.

Hanuman teaches us how to be brave and strong like him

Hanuman is the monkey God. He is the God of strength. He is very strong and clever. He can lift mountains. Sometimes Hanuman can be a bit naughty. Hindu children love to listen to the stories of Hanuman. It makes them want to be strong and courageous like him. It makes them want to do God's work and of course be a little naughty like him.

Krishna teaches us about the different ways of becoming spiritual

Krishna is another avatar of Vishnu born on earth to help us understand religion. He teaches how we can think about God in different ways and how we can find God using different methods. He teaches that we are all God's playmates, and are born on earth to take part in God's play. Krishna is shown with his partner Radha. Krishna is sometimes shown holding a flute. His hair is decorated with a peacock feather. Krishna's teachings about religion can be read in a book called the Gita.

Ganesh is the elephant-headed God who removes obstacles and brings good luck

Ganesh is the son of the Mother Goddess Parvati. While protecting his mummy, young Ganesh had to go into battle where his head was chopped off. To quickly save his life, the Mother Goddess had to replace his head with an elephant's head. Hindus always worship Ganesh first because he removes all obstacles and brings good luck. They worship him before they start anything new, like joining a school, or going on a journey, or celebrating a festival. Ganesh is not only brave, he is also very wise. Hindu children learn about the importance of being brave and wise from the stories of Ganesh.

God does not only live in heaven, He is here too

Hindus say that God not only lives in heaven, He is here too. They say that God has been in front of us all the time but we just did not realise it. It is God alone who appears as everything around us, like the galaxies, the planets, the plants, animals and human beings. **Brahman** is the special name Hindus give to God appearing as everything and everyone. This Brahman is seen most clearly in human beings and is called **Atman**. It is God alone who is looking out through the eyes of every living thing, and He shines most clearly in the eyes of all human beings.

God appearing as everything and everyone is called Brahman

This means that we have to take extra care in how we live. We should not hurt or harm anything or anyone, because God resides in all. We should take extra care of the plants, the animals and the environment. Everyone and everything should be treated with respect. Hinduism places a great deal of emphasis on preserving and looking after the environment as the whole world is an expression of Brahman.

God appearing in everyone is called Atman

Every human being is a spark of God. It is God who shines in the eyes of every living thing. God as our real Self is called Atman. If we make an effort to sit still and meditate to find out who we truly are, we discover that we are indeed a spark of God. We discover God as our real being, our true Self. This is why when Hindus greet others, they put their hands together and say **namaste**, which means: 'There is God in you.'

Story to explain how the same God can take on different names and forms

A student asked his teacher, 'How can the same God sometimes be Vishnu or Shiva or the Mother Goddess, or a God in another religion?' The teacher asked the student to come to his home the next day. In the meantime, the teacher bought lots of different shaped moulds for making ice in his freezer. Some moulds were like cubes, some were round and some were like stars. The next day when the student arrived, the teacher took out all the moulds from the freezer and from each, he took out differently shaped blocks of ice. Some looked like cubes, some like round balls, and some looked like stars. He then placed all of them in front of his student and asked if they were all different. The student said, 'Yes.'

The teacher then explained, 'Even though they look different, and you call them by different names like round, cube and star-shaped, they are really the same. They are all made out of water. The same water becomes frozen into different shapes. In the same way, the same God is called by different names. Some Hindus call God Vishnu, some call him Shiva, some like to think of God as the Mother Goddess. People of other religions have their own different names for God.

This story explains how Hindus think of the same one God in different ways. The same God is given different names by other religions too. Even though the names and forms of God are different, it is still the same God that all religions adore.

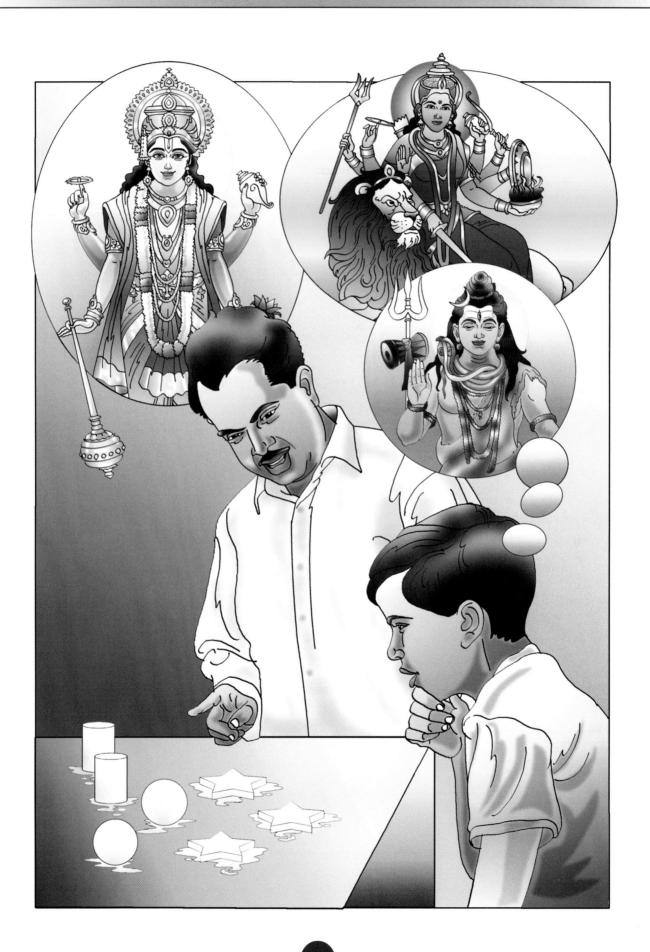

Learning about Religion

* Pluralism: Hinduism is a pluralistic religion; it offers many different ways of thinking about God. God is given different names depending on the role He or She plays. For example:
    * Brahma is God in the role of the creator.
    * Vishnu is God in the role of the preserver.
    * Shiva is God in the role of both the creator and destroyer.
    * Shakti is the name of God as female. She can appear in many forms like Parvati, Durga, Saraswati or Lakshmi.
* Avatars are God descending to earth in human form to help mankind become religious. Two examples of Avatars are Rama and Krishna
* Ganesh: the elephant headed God who removes obstacles and brings good luck
* Hanuman: the monkey faced God who is the God of strength and intelligence
* Brahman: God appearing as everything and everyone
* Atman: God appearing as our essential Self
* Namaste means, there is God in you

Learning from Religion

* How is pluralism different from polytheism (which believes in many almighty Gods)?
* Why is pluralism so important in modern times when people of different religions have to learn to live with each other?
* Is it good to say that one religion is better than another, or to ask people to change their religion?
* God as a Mother; is this better than God as a Father?
* Instead of saying that God is loving, and truthful would it be better to say that truth and love are better names for God?
* How can thinking about God as our real self be useful?

Classroom Activities:
- ❖ Visit the Hinduism for schools website and download outline drawings of Hindu Gods and Goddesses to paint. Use different colours to highlight their roles and special features
- ❖ Two methods to explain pluralism:
  1. Everyone is given a piece of play-dough to shape into their ideal image of God. Though all figures look very different they are all made from the same building material
  2. Ask a person to sit in the centre of the room and let everyone describe him. Notice the variation in the way the same person is described depending on the angle from which he is viewed. The same is true with different religions. Some may address God as their father in heaven, and some may address God as their mother in heaven.
- ❖ Reflecting on the idea of Atman: Are we special? What makes us special? Is it just our appearance and our abilities, or is there something more to us?
- ❖ Discuss how the idea of Atman gives a good reason why we should be fair to others and treat everyone and everything with dignity

Chapter 3
Hindu holy books

Hinduism teaches that the best way we can learn about God is from people who have actually experienced God. We can ask them to help us learn about God. But it is very difficult to find such people. The second best way to find out about God is by studying what these people have said about God. This information has been recorded in holy books called the scriptures.

Hinduism has two types of holy books or scriptures

The first type of books are called the Vedas

The Vedas are considered very important in Hinduism because they tell us how the rishis felt when they experienced God. The Vedas tell us how we can experience God for ourselves. The Vedas were first written in a very ancient language called **Sanskrit**. Veda in Sanskrit means knowledge. So the Vedas are books of knowledge about God.

The Upanishads are parts of the Vedas that are very special. The Upanishads tell us how everything and everyone is connected to God. They tell us that the essential nature of everything including ourselves is something very special called the Spirit or Brahman.

The Gita is another important holy book of the Hindus. It teaches how we can relate to God in different ways, and how we can use different pathways to reach God. Some people find God through prayer and worship, some by doing good deeds, and some reach God by meditating. We can use any of these ways to find God or invent our own special way to reach God.

A Story from the Vedas

Once, a young boy went to see a rishi to learn about God. He asked the rishi, 'How can I find God?' The rishi replied, 'Find out who you truly are, because even though you don't know it, you are actually God.'

The boy thought for a long time. He looked at his body and thought: 'This body must be me. So does that mean that my body is God?' But then he realised that his body cannot be God, because the body is certain to die one day, and God cannot die!

Then he decided to find out who he truly was, because that is what the rishi had asked him to do. He sat down to meditate to search for his true Self. After sitting in meditation for a very long time he had a strange and thrilling experience. Even though his eyes were closed, he saw a brilliant light. The light he saw was more brilliant than the light of the sun. He did not feel dazzled, in fact he felt very excited. He could see the brilliant light everywhere, even though his eyes were closed. He could also hear the Om sound that seemed to be coming from everywhere.

He then tried to move his body, but he could not feel his body! He suddenly realised that he was *not* the body. He was really the brilliant light that was everywhere. This was the most exciting thing the boy had ever experienced. By trying to find out who he truly was, he had experienced God.

When the boy finished his meditation, he could feel his body again. But now he was no longer an ordinary boy; he was the boy who had experienced God in meditation. He had turned into a rishi.

This is what the Vedas teach, 'God lies hidden in everything, including all living things, and in us. Through meditation, we can find God within us as our innermost Self or Atman.'

The second type of holy books of the Hindus contain epics and legends

The second type of holy books of the Hindus, contain lots of very exciting and colourful stories. They include epics like the **Ramayana** and **Mahabharata**. They also include books called the **Puranas** which contain legendary stories about Gods and Goddesses. Such stories teach Hindu children how to tell the difference between what is right and what is wrong, what is good and what is bad. Such stories, emphasise the importance of honesty, courage, discipline and being helpful to others.

The Ramayana

This epic relates the famous story of Rama and his wife Sita. It narrates why Rama and Sita left their kingdom and went to live in the forest, where a wicked king kidnapped Sita. Rama destroyed the wicked king and rescued Sita with the help of his friend Hanuman the monkey God. They came back to their kingdom where a big celebration took place. The day they returned is still celebrated as the festival of Diwali. Rama and Sita became the king and queen and ruled very wisely. Like Rama, all Hindus like to be brave and just. Like Sita, all Hindu women like to be gentle, kind and loyal. Hindu children are taught to be strong, brave and helpful like Hanuman.

The Mahabharata

This is the famous story of five brave princes. They were called the Pandavas. They had one hundred evil cousins who were very jealous of them. The evil cousins kept trying to take away the Pandavas' kingdom, but Krishna helped the Pandava brothers to fight back and regain their kingdom. The Mahabharata teaches Hindus how to lead a religious life.

A short story from the Mahabharata

The Pandava brothers had been sent to live in the forest by their evil cousins. One day, the eldest Pandava went to drink some water from a pool. The pool was guarded by a divine being. Before he could drink the water, he heard the divine being saying, 'You may only drink the water from this pool if you can answer my questions. If you drink this water without giving the correct answers, you will die.' The Pandava prince was very wise. He did not mind answering difficult questions.

The divine being asked:
'What saves man from all dangers?' The prince replied: 'Courage rescues man from all dangers'. The divine being was very pleased with this answer.

He asked a second question:
'Who is man's best friend?' The prince replied, 'A man's best friend should be his wife and a woman's best friend should be her husband. If husband and wife live together like best friends, then everyone, including their children, benefit.'

The divine being asked the next question:
'What is the best thing we possess?' The prince replied, 'The best thing we possess is our character. We must develop an upright character. Possessing other things is less important.

The divine being asked the final question:
'How can we give up something and still be truly rich? The prince replied, 'As long as we keep on asking for more and more things, we cannot call ourselves truly rich. Only when we become content with what we have, and give up desires for more and more things do we become truly rich. The divine being was very pleased with all the wise answers, and let the Pandava prince drink the water and go on his way.

A story from the Purana

Once, Ganesh and his brother Kartikeya decided to have a race. It was decided that the brother who could go round the universe and return first will be declared the winner. Kartikeya had a pet peacock who could travel at the speed of light. He jumped on it and zoomed off into space. Ganesh's pet was a little mouse, who was quite plump and slow. Ganesh asked his father and mother Shiva and Parvati to sit together. He then bowed down to them and started to walk round them with his mouse. After he had gone round once he stopped, bowed down to his parents and sat down. After a long time Kartikeya returned, huffing and puffing. When he saw Ganesh already there he was surprised. 'You have not been round the universe,' he exclaimed. 'I have been round the universe,' said Ganesh and asked, 'Is it not God who appears as the whole universe?' Kartikeya said, 'Yes, so what?' 'Well here sits God as Shiva and Parvati, I went round them, that means I have been round the universe,' explained Ganesh. 'He is right,' laughed Parvati. 'He has won the race by using his intelligence.'

Learning about Religion

❖ The Vedas are the books of knowledge about God
❖ Sanskrit is the ancient language of India
❖ The Gita teaches about many different ways to think about and find God
❖ The Puranas contain stories of Hindu Gods and Goddesses
❖ The Ramayana is the epic story of Rama, Sita and Hanuman
❖ The Mahabharata is the story of the five Pandava princes who were helped by Krishna

Learning from Religion

❖ Why are holy books important in every religion?
❖ Why are books still the second best way to learn about God?
❖ Why are there two types of holy book in Hinduism?
❖ What are the holy books of other religions and how do they compare with the holy books of the Hindus?
❖ Can any holy book contain all the knowledge of God?
❖ Can words truly describe God? Can poetry help?
❖ Can there be modern scriptures?

Classroom Activities

❖ Dress up as different characters of the Puranas (Vishnu, Shiva, Rama, Sita, Krishna, Mother Goddesses)
❖ Make masks of Hanuman or Ganesh. Images can be downloaded from our website
❖ Write up stories about Gods and Goddesses and then act them out
❖ Use digital recording equipment to produce short films of these plays
❖ Write poems describing God
❖ Download religious music; write and perform a religious musical

Chapter 4
What Hindus believe

We are born again and again

Hindus say that we do not have only one life; we have many lives and continue to be born again and again. This is called **Samsar**, the cycle of birth and death. Our body grows old, gets worn out and finally dies. But our soul continues to live. After a while, the soul takes on a new birth. Between births it may create a mental heaven or hell for itself and spend some time there, but then it occupies a new body. This is called reincarnation.

Why don't we remember our past lives?

Even though most people cannot remember their past lives, there are some children who are able to recall their past lives and give all sorts of details about their past life, with names and places and dates. In some cases, the information they give about a past life can be checked out and has been found to be accurate. Scientists are puzzled by this and are not able to explain this, except to say that it may be because of reincarnation.

Taking re-birth is like changing jumpers

Imagine you have a brand new jumper. You love this jumper. You wear it all the time. After some time, it starts to wear out. It gets torn. Soon you don't want to wear this jumper any more. It has become old and tattered. You throw it away and your parents buy you a new jumper. Reincarnation is a bit like that. We discard our old bodies because they have become old and diseased; we then take birth in a new body.

Is there no end to the cycle of re-birth?

Do we keep being reborn forever?
Being born again and again is a bit like going round on a merry-go-round. It is fun at the start, but then after many rounds, it can become boring. Hindus say that in the same way, we also get bored with being born again and again, and look for a way out. A person looking for a way out is said to be looking for **moksha**. A person can only stop being born again and again when he finds out that he is one with God. Once a person finds that out, he loses all interest in being born again.

A story from the Upanishad:
Nachiketa and the king of death

Once upon a time in ancient India lived a clever little boy called Nachiketa. He wanted to learn about everything. He would keep asking his father difficult questions. One day, the boy asked his father, 'What happens to us when we die?' The father did not know the answer. He became annoyed, and told the boy, 'Go to the king of death and ask him such questions!' Of course, the father had only said this in anger. He did not mean that the boy should actually die and go to the king of death, but that is how it sounded.

The story goes: Nachiketa went to Yama, the king of death. He wanted to find out about death. He wondered why everyone had to die and what happens to us after we die. He asked Yama to tell him the secret of death.

Yama was very pleased with this clever boy who was so curious to find out about death. He told Nachiketa the secret of death. He told him, 'The truth is that we never die. Only our bodies die, we continue to live. The reason why the body has to die is because it becomes old or ill. After the body dies, we are reborn in a new body and this keeps happening again and again. Nachiketa asked, 'But does this mean that there is no end to this cycle of rebirth, are we are trapped forever?' Yama replied, 'When we become tired of being born again and again, we look for a way out. The way out is to find God. After we find God, there is no need to be born again, because God is so attractive that we merge in God. Becoming one with God is called **Yoga**.' Nachiketa was very pleased to learn about the secret of death. Yama sent Nachiketa back to his family, where he taught the secret of death to others.

The Law of Karma

Another important thing Hindus believe in is called the law of karma. This law says that everything we do will produce certain results. For example, if we work hard at school, we get good results. If we do not work hard, we get poor results. Everything we do adds up and produces good or bad, or mixed results. This is why we have to be very careful about everything we do. Sometimes the results of what we do catch up immediately, sometimes they take a long time to catch up with us. This is why people sometimes use the phrase *my Karma is catching up with me.* If we act very badly, it is not God who punishes us, but the law of karma catching up with us and making us pay a price for the bad things we may have done.

Imagine that you have a test in school tomorrow. You have a lot of studying to do. But then your favourite TV programme is just about to start. You really want to see that programme, but if you don't do your revision, you will do badly in the test. You choose to do the revision. The next day, you do well in your test. You feel pleased with yourself. You had a choice between watching TV or doing revision. You chose well, and good results followed. You were in charge of what you did. The law of karma then rewarded you.

Ahimsa is one of the most important things Hindus believe in

It teaches that we must do our best not to hurt or harm anything or anybody. It also teaches us that we must treat everyone and everything with a great deal of respect.

Why should we not hurt or harm anything?

Hinduism teaches that God (or spirit) shines in the eyes of every living thing including our own, so when we hurt anyone we are actually hurting ourselves. This is why it is very foolish to needlessly hurt other living beings. Instead of hurting other living things, we should show respect for all living things, because it is the same God (or spirit) that lives in all of us.

The story of Ganesh and the cat

Ganesh is the son of the Mother Goddess. Like all children, he was sent to school to become clever. On the first day, he learnt the first three letters of the alphabet: A, B, C. He was very excited when he came home. He ran to his mummy saying, 'Mummy, mummy play with me.' But mummy was busy. She asked him to play by himself in the garden. Ganesh went into the garden, and there he saw the neighbour's cat. Ganesh said, 'Cat, play with me. We are going to play the game of School. I am going to be the teacher, and you will be my student. I will teach you the alphabet.' In wobbly writing he wrote on the board: 'A B C'. Then he pointed at 'A' and said to the cat, 'Repeat after me, A..' The cat just went 'Meow.' Ganesh said, 'Cat: that is not very clever. Repeat after me: 'A, B...' The cat went 'Meow, Meow....' Ganesh was getting annoyed with the cat. He said, 'Cat! You must learn the alphabet properly, otherwise I will have to punish you!' He then pointed at the letters on the board and said, 'Repeat after me: A B C...' The cat went 'Meow, Meow, Meow.' Ganesh became angry. He picked up the cat and smacked it. The cat did not like this game anymore, and ran away. Ganesh thought he would go back into his home. When he returned, he was shocked to see his mummy covered in bruises. Ganesh loved his mummy, he said, 'Mummy! Who has hurt you mummy? Mummy said, 'Come here my boy, and tell me, what were you doing just now?' Ganesh said, 'I was just playing in the garden with the cat.' Mummy asked, 'Did you hurt the cat?' Ganesh thought oh oh! He replied, 'Just a little.' The Mother Goddess said, 'Listen to me my boy, and listen carefully. This is the most important lesson you will learn in your life. I, the Mother Goddess, am the mother of the whole universe, and live in everything. It is I who live in the cat, so when you hurt the cat, you hurt me my boy. Do you now understand who has hurt me?' Ganesh now understood. It is God alone who lives in all living things, so if we hurt or harm anything, we hurt God. From that day on, Ganesh would never hurt any living thing.

Just like Ganesh, we must also remember not to hurt or harm anyone or anything. God lives in everything and in everyone. We must take great care of everything, including the earth, the plants, the animals, and especially all human beings.

What should we do if someone tries to hurt us?

Once upon a time there lived a very poisonous snake. This snake lived near a small village and used to bite and kill people of the village. Everyone in the village was frightened of the snake. One day, a holy man passed by. He saw how everyone was scared of the snake. He went to the snake and advised him to give up his evil ways and lead a good life. The snake liked the holy man and what he said made a lot of sense, so from that day on, it stopped biting or attacking the villagers.

After some time, the people of the village saw that the snake had changed. It was not biting anymore. Everyone felt happy. But some villagers were not very nice. When they found out that the snake would not bite, they went after the snake and stamped on it and hit it with clubs. The snake remembered what the wise man had taught about not hurting anyone so he just kept quiet and suffered. After some time the wise man returned to the village. He went to visit the snake and saw the poor snake bruised and bleeding. The snake said, 'O wise man, you told me not to bite, I listened to your advice and see what has happened to me?'

The wise man said, 'Oh, foolish snake, I told you not to bite, but I never told you to stop hissing, if someone comes to harm you. If you had just hissed, you would have been safe from evil people. Hiss but do not bite. Then you can live happily and safely.'

Like the snake, we have to hiss to protect ourselves. If someone tries to bully us, we must not suffer in silence. We must make a fuss and let everyone know about the bullying. This is like hissing but not biting in order to protect ourselves.

Should we stand up against injustice?

The law of karma teaches that if we ignore doing something that needs doing, then we have acquired bad karma and will have to bear the consequences of 'not doing something.' If we see **injustice** and do not stand up against it, then we acquire bad karma. Krishna taught that we have to stand up against injustice. Where possible, we must try and find a way out without resorting to violence. For example, **Gandhi** was able to gain independence for India without using violence. In many cases, it is possible to resolve serious disputes without using violence.

Learning about Religion
- ❖ Samsara means the cycle of birth and death
- ❖ Moksha means freedom from the cycle of rebirth
- ❖ The Law of Karma teaches that we have to bear the consequences of everything we do (sometimes what we forgot to do)
- ❖ Ahimsa means not to hurt or harm anyone or anything
- ❖ Vandalising the environment is violence against nature

Learning from Religion
- ❖ Can we actually live without hurting or harming other living things?
- ❖ Is it better to be a vegetarian?
- ❖ How can our belief in life after death influence the way we live?
- ❖ How does the Hindu idea of life after death compare with the idea of life after death in other religions?
- ❖ How can we show our respect for the environment?
- ❖ How can religious teachings help us fight global warming?

Classroom Activities
- ❖ Putting Ahimsa into practice:
  Set up a weekly Ahimsa chart for all students
  Minus points if they hurt or harm others;
  Plus points if they are helpful to others
- ❖ Set up the practice of recycling in your school
  Encourage your family to recycle
- ❖ Download the game: *Moksha* from our website
  The game is an interesting way to learn about the Law of Karma, Ahimsa, Samsara & Moksha

Chapter 5
Worship and Celebration

Worship is called Puja

Hindus can worship God in many different forms. Some worship Vishnu, some Shiva, some Rama, some Krishna and some worship God as the Mother Goddess. Worship is carried out in front of an image (called **Murti**) of their chosen form of God, called the **deity**. The worship ceremony is called **puja.**

Puja (or prayers) in the home

The image of God is placed in a little shrine in the home. The image is decorated, mainly with flowers. Water is sprinkled in the shrine room to make everything pure. A mark or tilak is made on the forehead with coloured powder. This helps people focus their minds on God. At the start of the worship, a lamp is lit in front of the image. It is a way of asking God to lead us from ignorance to light. Food is offered to the image to show gratitude to God for everything he has given us. An incense stick is lit, which gives out a sweet scent. Sometimes a little bell is rung during the worship ceremony. It helps to block out other disturbing sounds. The lamp, or sometimes the incense stick, is waved gently in front of the image. This is called the **arati**. It is a way of welcoming God into the home. After this, the family members may sit in front of the image and sing hymns or holy songs. They may read from the scriptures, or sit quietly and meditate on God. Some may tell beads and repeat the name of God. At the end of the worship, everyone bows to the deity. The food that was offered in the beginning is now shared and eaten by everyone. This sanctified food is called **prashad.**

How do we feel when we do daily puja?

During the puja ceremony, all our senses are engaged and directed towards God. Our eyes see the image of God and the lighted lamps; our noses smell the lovely scent from the flowers and incense. Our ears hear the tinkling sound of the bell and the hymns being sung, and we can feel the beads while we are repeating the name of God. We also get a chance to eat the prashad. The puja ceremony engages all our senses and directs our mind towards God. This routine gives us a break from daily chores and allows us to think of higher things. We feel calm and happy at the end of the ceremony.

Puja at the Temple

Hindus think of the temple or **mandir** as the home of God on earth. People go to the temple so that they can see the image of God. This is called **darshan**. An offering of flowers or fruits may be taken to the temple. Shoes are left at the entrance to keep the temple clean. A bell at the entrance may be rung to announce one's presence. Devotees bow to the image of God at the centre of the temple, and to other deities placed on the surrounding walls. People are seen walking around the central deity, always keeping the deity on the right hand side. The congregation takes part in the arati ceremony. When the arati hymns are sung, everyone joins in. The singing is sometimes accompanied by musical instruments. At the end of the ceremony, the arati tray is passed around, and people cup their hands over the arati flame to receive God's blessings. At the time of leaving, everyone gets some prashad to eat.

How do we feel when we visit the temple?

Going to the temple, is like visiting the home of our real father and mother, who is God. The sight of the majestic temple reminds us about the majesty of God. The centre of the temple is called **garbha-griha.** The image of the main deity is kept here. When the devotees catch sight of the image they feel satisfied, they feel that they have actually seen God. When so many devotees meet up at the temple either for the worship ceremony or to celebrate festivals, they feel nice because they feel they belong to a larger family.

Home alone: the story of the boy who fed God

A long time ago in India, lived a little boy called Raj. Once, Raj's parents had to go out of town. Raj was left, home alone. Before his parents left, they instructed Raj not to eat his breakfast until he had fed the family deity, Shiva. Raj promised to feed Shiva before eating his breakfast. In the morning Raj remembered his promise. He could not have his breakfast until he did the puja and fed Shiva. He brought flowers and food and laid them out in front of the image of Shiva. He copied exactly what his parents used to do: he sprinkled water round the shrine, tinkled the little bell and waved the incense stick in front of the image. Then he waited for Shiva to start eating the food that he had offered. He waited and waited for Shiva to start eating, but Shiva did not come. A long time passed and nothing happened. Raj was feeling hungry, but he remembered his promise. He could not eat until Shiva had been fed. He was getting a bit annoyed with Shiva, so he told Shiva gently, 'Don't be naughty, come and eat your food!' Still, Shiva did not come. He thought that perhaps he should tell Shiva off, then he would listen. So he said, 'Be a good boy and eat your breakfast, otherwise I will thump you!' Still nothing happened…Now Raj began to feel very hungry. He felt like crying but he was a brave little boy, so he held back his tears. He said, 'Oh Shiva! Why don't you eat? Is it because I am a little boy who does not know how to do proper puja?' Poor Raj! Finally he just could not help himself and burst into tears.

Suddenly, to his surprise, he heard a voice, 'I will eat the food, but don't thump me!' To his amazement, he saw Shiva sitting in front of him, eating up all the food that he had offered. Raj was overjoyed! After Shiva had eaten, he disappeared and Raj could have his breakfast. When Raj's parents came home, he told them how difficult it had been to feed Shiva. Raj's parents were amazed. They said, 'Raj! God actually came and ate the food you offered!! How fantastic!'

God is not bothered if we can or cannot perform a complicated puja ceremony. He just looks in our hearts to see if we love him dearly or not. If we love him dearly then He will reveal himself to us.

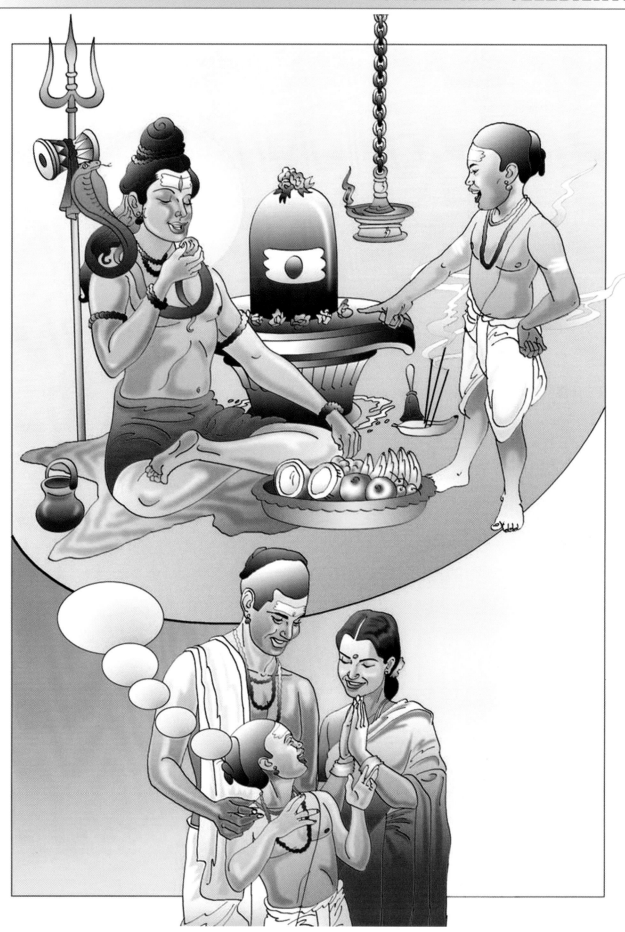

Festivals are a time to celebrate

Festivals are a good way of reminding people about the importance of God and religion. Families and community members dress up in their best clothes and get together at homes and in temples. There may be many events taking place on festival dates. Some adults may fast on some festival days, but normally the festival ends with a feast for everyone.

Diwali: the festival of light

Diwali is the most famous Hindu festival. It is called the festival of light because people celebrate this festival by lighting lots of little lamps. The word diva means lamp, and Diwali means a row of lamps. Diwali occurs in winter and helps to light up the dark winter nights with lots of lamps and firework displays.

The reason for lighting up lamps during Diwali goes back to the story of the Ramayana. When Rama and Sita returned to their city in the middle of the night, it was very dark and they could not see their way home. In order to show their love for Rama and Sita, the people of the city lit up the whole city with lots of little lamps. Even though this happened a very long time ago, people still remember this special day and light lamps and celebrate the home-coming of Rama and Sita.

Holi celebrates the arrival of spring

Holi is called the festival of colours, because everything looks colourful with the arrival of spring. Hindus celebrate Holi by sprinkling coloured water and coloured powder on each other and having lots of fun. There is a story associated with Holi. Thousands of years ago, there was a little boy called Prahlad. He loved Vishnu very much. But a demoness called Holika wanted to kill Prahlad. Vishnu rescued the boy and destroyed the demoness on this day. In the evening, a bonfire is lit and coconuts are offered to the fire to celebrate the destruction of Holika.

Nine nights of worshipping the Mother Goddess is celebrated as Navaratri

Navaratri is the festival of nine nights. It occurs in winter. People get together and pray to the Mother Goddess. They dance in a circle around an image of the Mother Goddess. The story goes that the Mother Goddess fought a demon during these nine nights. On the tenth night, she destroyed the demon. The tenth night is very special and is called **Dusherra**. Special prayers are offered to the Mother Goddess during the Navaratri period.

Pilgrimage

A pilgrimage is a religious journey for visiting holy places and meeting holy people and doing charitable work. Places where holy people may have lived, become places of pilgrimage. Mountains like the Himalayas or rivers like the Ganges also become places of pilgrimage, because they are beautiful locations where our minds naturally think of higher things.

The story of the holy river Ganga (Ganges)

A long time ago in the heavens, lived a beautiful Goddess called Ganga. She was very playful, very powerful and very pure. Everything she touched became pure like her. A king on earth wanted to bring her down to earth so that she could purify everyone. Finally, Ganga agreed to come down, but she came down from heaven with such force that she would have shattered the earth. Lord Shiva had to step in and catch her in his hair to slow her flow. Hindus say that everyone who takes a dip in the river Ganga becomes purified by her holy touch.

Why should we bother with religious rituals and ceremonies?

Daily reminder: The reason why rituals are important is because they keep reminding us about our religion and God. If we did not do some kind of daily ritual like worship or prayer or meditation, we could easily forget about God and religion.

Discipline: We can never succeed in any activity unless we exercise discipline. We cannot do well in our studies or sports or art or music if we do not put in a lot of effort and cultivate discipline. The same is true of religion: rituals are a kind of discipline. Apart from doing the puja ceremony, there are other kinds of disciplines like fasting. On special days, some Hindus will fast, some may only eat fruit, and some may only have one meal on that day. There are many other kinds of disciplines like meditating or doing yoga exercises everyday. Some Hindus may visit temples or go on pilgrimages.

Symbolic reasons for doing rituals: As God is difficult to see or experience in person, we do the next best thing: we create an image of God, called a murti. Though these images or symbols are not God, we can still link to God through such images and symbols. Because these images are so important, they are treated with a great deal of respect. Though most of the religious ceremonies are symbolic gestures, they are useful and necessary to focus our minds on God.

The Law of Karma teaches that everything we do produces some consequences, hence doing rituals like puja or visiting temples or going on pilgrimage are bound to produce beneficial results. Even though Hinduism does not impose hard and fast rules about any ritual like visiting the temple everyday, it encourages rituals as they are expected to produce good results in days to come.

Learning about Religion

❖ Puja is the worship ceremony
❖ A mandir is a temple; the home of God on earth
❖ The arati is a ceremony to welcome God in to the home or temple
❖ Darshan means seeing God's image
❖ Prashad is the food distributed and eaten by devotees after it has been offered to God
❖ Diwali is the festival of lights to mark the return of Rama and Sita
❖ Holi marks the arrival of spring; it is called the festival of colours
❖ Navaratri celebrates nine nights of worshipping the Mother Goddess
❖ Ganga is the name of a holy river that purifies all who take a dip in it

Learning from Religion

❖ Why bother with any rituals or religious ceremonies?
❖ What is the role of prayer? How often should we pray or visit a temple?
❖ Are festivals just an excuse for a party?
❖ How do festivals celebrated with the family and community help us understand our religion better?
❖ Compare the festivals of other religions. What are the similarities and differences?

Classroom Activities

❖ Visit a local Hindu temple and observe worship, taking notes of everything you observe and things that come to your attention. If allowed, take photos or make a video recording

❖ Ask a Hindu student or a Hindu parent to help make a temporary shrine, install a deity and carry out a worship ceremony. Offer fruit to God and share out the food as prashad

❖ Arrange to celebrate a Hindu festival like Diwali, Holi or Navaratri in the class or school. Visit our website to get some ideas

❖ Make an Indian rice pudding, called payasam. The recipe can be found on our website

❖ Make a power-point presentation on why and how Diwali is celebrated

❖ Write a diary imagining you are Rama or Sita returning to Ayodhya

❖ Write an essay about how we feel when we visit any holy place

❖ Describe the sights and sounds and how we felt

❖ Can we call these feelings spiritual?

Chapter 6
Can we see God?

Three views about belief in God and Religion
(1) Atheists are people who do not believe in God or Religion. They argue, 'How can we believe in God when we cannot see him? Or how can a loving, almighty God allow the suffering we see all around us?' Either he is not almighty or he is not so loving!

(2) Agnostics are people who are not sure about God. They argue that they do not have enough reason to believe in God, or enough reason not to believe in God.

(3) Theists are people who believe in a loving, almighty, all-knowing God. They believe that He is responsible for creating and looking after the universe. Most Hindus are theists, and believe in God as a grand personality like Vishnu or Shiva or the Mother Goddess. However there are some Hindus who do not like to think of God like an almighty person living in heaven, but as their own inner-most Self called **Atman**. These Hindus think that it is better to think of God as *that* which holds everything and everyone together called **Brahman**. When one thinks of God as a principle rather than a personality, the question of how can God allow suffering does not arise.

Can we prove God?
Hindus say that it is not possible to prove God just by thinking hard about it or arguing about it. The only proper way to know if God exists is to experience God for ourselves. It is not good to believe in God just because someone says so. We have to make an effort to experience God for ourselves. We should work hard here and now while we are alive, to find him. This is what the saints of all world religions did, they discovered God. We have to do the same.

Learn to find God from people who have seen God
In order to find God, it is good to learn about God from prophets who have experienced God, but it is difficult to find them as many of them lived a long time ago.

Learn about God from the scriptures

The next best way to learn about God is to study the lives and teachings of the prophets so that we can follow in their footsteps and find God. What some of these holy people taught about God has been preserved in the scriptures. It is useful to read these as a guidance to find God for ourselves.

Can books describe or explain God?

Hinduism says that these books are useful, but God cannot be properly described or explained through the words of any holy book. Just as when we experience something truly awesome, we struggle to find the right words to describe it; God too is so awesome that no words of any book can truly describe him. Poetry has a way of describing things that are difficult to put in words. Hence the Upanishads of the Hindus use poetry to talk about God.

We have to experience God for ourselves

The only way we can really be sure about God is to experience Him for ourselves. Prophets and scriptures can be helpful, but then we must go further and make an effort to find God for ourselves. Belief is a good starting point in a religious journey but the journey has to end with first hand experience.

Has anyone experienced God in recent times?

Some recent Hindu saints like Tulsi, Meera or Narsi have seen God as a person like Vishnu or Shiva or the Mother Goddess or as Rama or Krishna. Raman Maharshi who lived about 50 years ago, experienced God as the Atman, our innermost Self. Vivekananda who lived about a hundred years ago could experience God in everything and everyone. He experienced God as Brahman.

The Story of a little prince who was determined to see God

The name of this prince was Dhruva. His mother, the queen, told him lots of stories about God. Dhruva loved these stories. He particularly liked the stories about God as Vishnu. One day, his mother, who was a very wise queen, told Dhruva: 'You know, the king is not your real father. Your real father is God. Everyone's real father is God.' Dhruva was thrilled to hear that everyone's real father was God. Dhruva started to think: 'If my real father is God, I have to see Him.' He told his mother, 'I want to see my real father.' The queen replied: 'It is very difficult to find God. Only a few people ever bother to look for Him. They go to the forest, sit under a tree and repeat the name of God for many years. Even then only a few succeed in seeing God. You are too young to worry about such things.' Dhruva was not happy with such an answer. Even though he was only five years old, he was determined to find God. In the middle of the night, he slipped away from the palace and walked into the forest. There he found a large tree close to a river. He sat under the tree to meditate and to repeat the name of God as Vishnu.

The brave little prince kept repeating the name Vishnu for many days and months. But Vishnu did not appear. The little boy was determined, now he started repeating the name of God in the night as well as in the day. Still, Vishnu did not come. The little prince was determined to see God. He asked Vishnu, "Is it just because I am a little boy that you are not showing yourself to me?" The next moment he saw a brilliant light, and in front of him, stood Vishnu in all his glory. The little boy was thrilled. Seeing God is the most exciting thing that can happen to us. God appears more brilliant than anything we have ever seen. Everything else appears dull and boring after we see God. Vishnu told Dhruva, "My boy, you are very special to me. Even though you are so young, you were determined to see me. Now you must go back to your palace. In days to come, you will become a famous king who will rule wisely and teach people how to find God. I name the star at the north-pole after you. Like you, it is also very steadfast and determined; it always stays in the same place in the sky." Since that time the Hindus call the north-pole star Dhruva.

This story illustrates that it is possible to see God as a person. The love of the devotee makes God take on the form of the devotee's choice, and appear in front of him. In the case of Dhruva, God showed himself to him as Vishnu.

The Story of a young man who found God in our times

About a hundred years ago lived a young man called Naren. Ever since he was a little boy, he loved to listen to stories about God. When he was a bit older he began to realise that most of the stories about God were just made-up stories and could not be for real. This got him worried. 'Maybe God is not for real, he is just made-up,' he thought. The other thought that worried young Naren was, 'If God is really all-powerful and all-loving, why does He allow all the suffering we see around us? Surely he can click his fingers and make sure that no one suffers even for a moment. So why doesn't He do that?'

'How can I be sure that God is real?' thought Naren. Surely someone must have seen Him.' He started visiting all the holy men and asking them, 'Have you seen God?' To his surprise none of the holy men confirmed that they had seen God. This got Naren even more worried. No one seems to have seen God, and yet everyone believes in Him. Naren changed his mind about God. He did not believe in God any more. His uncle told him to visit a holy man called Ramakrishna who would be able to give him a proper answer. Naren visited him and asked, 'Have you seen God?' Surprisingly Ramakrishna replied, 'Yes, I can see God even now as I see you, but he appears much clearer than you. I can show Him to you.' Naren had never met anyone who said that he could see God clearly all the time. Naren felt very happy; he decided to make the holy man his guru (teacher) so that he could see God. After spending many years with Ramakrishna, Naren was able to see God for himself. He could actually see that it was God who appeared as everything and everyone. This is one of the most exciting ways of experiencing God, all around us. Naren became very famous as Swami Vivekananda.

He taught that the best way to see God is to see Him in all living things and the best way to worship God is to serve mankind. He taught that the only way we can be sure about God is to experience God for ourselves.

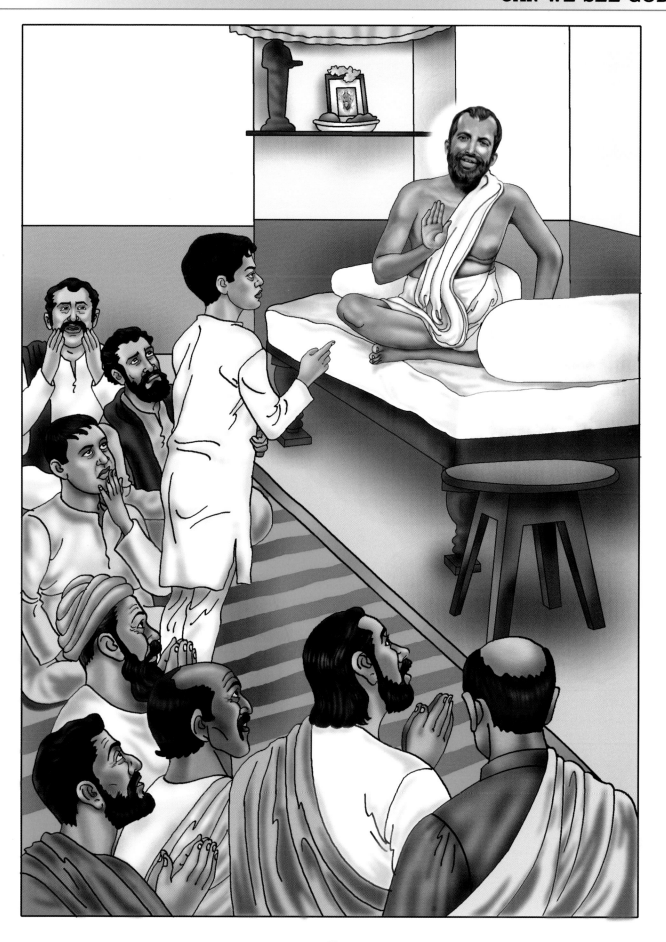

Who are we, and how are we linked with God?

When we look at ourselves in the mirror, we may think that we are the body we can see. We sometimes think that we are what our minds tell us we are. The mind offers us all sorts of thoughts about what we are: happy or sad, clever or not so clever, kind or unkind etc. We seem to be made up of our bodies and minds. But our minds and bodies are changing all the time. The body gets older and dies, the mind keeps shifting all the time. Hinduism teaches that our real Self is neither the body nor the mind, but something very special called the Spirit that shows up through our bodies and minds. Our real Self gets mixed up with the body and mind it experiences and loses sight of its real nature, which is the Spirit. Through meditation, we can discover who we truly are. It is then that we make the amazing discovery that we are very special. We are the Spirit (Atman), God.

Why should we be moral?

Most people are frightened off by the suggestion that our essential Self is God. Some people fear that such ideas may make us big-headed. But that is not true because we also learn that everyone else is essentially God too. In a way this idea, that we are all connected with each other and with God, makes us behave better towards each other. This gives us the best reason for being **moral**. The reason why we should not hurt or harm anyone else is because unknowingly we are harming ourselves. The reason why we should help each other is also very easy to appreciate; essentially we are helping ourselves!

How do Hindus explain suffering?

In the Hindu religion there is no Devil. So he cannot be blamed for causing suffering. Hindus say that we are essentially spiritual beings (Atman); when we try and express ourselves in a physical manner (through the body) we pay a price for it. The price is suffering. The reason why we go, 'Ouch,' and pull our hand out of the fire is because our body is sending us a sharp message to make us move our hand away from the fire. The reason why we get pangs of hunger is because, in order to survive, the body is sending us an urgent message to feed ourselves. Suffering is the survival mechanism of the body. Another kind of suffering can be mental suffering. This arises because of unfulfilled desires. The only way we can overcome our desires is to realise that we are one with God. Then all desires and suffering vanish.

Learning about Religion

* Atheists do not believe in God or religion
* Agnostics are not sure if there is a God or not
* Theists believe in an almighty, all-knowing, all-loving God, who creates and looks after the universe
* Atman is God as our essential nature
* Brahman is God as the spiritual basis to everything and everyone
* The only proof of God in Hinduism is experiencing God for oneself
* Suffering is the price we pay for trying to express ourselves in a material way

Learning from Religion

* How can belief in God or the Self influence the way we live?
* How would this be different from the way a Humanist lives?
* Investigate how the same God can be:
  (1) Like a grand person?
  (2) As our real Self (Atman)?
  (3) As the essential part of everything and everyone (Brahman)?
* The importance of common-sense in making sense of the world and God
* Do we think that there can be a God even though we see so much suffering in the world?

Classroom Activities

* Compare the God experience of holy people of different religions
* Discuss: Belief is just the starting point in a religious journey
* List reasons why:
  - Atheists do not believe in God
  - Agnostics are not sure about God
  - Theists believe in God
* Write an essay on: Is God for real or just an invention like Santa Claus?
* Discuss: People suffer because it is their own fault
* Discuss: Does science have all the answers?
* Discuss: People are not evil, they are just misguided

Chapter 7
Life and Death

Different views on what happens after we die

Atheists are people who do not believe in a soul or God or religion. Hence they do not believe that we are reborn. They say that there is only one life, the one that we have now. We must make the most of it rather than worry about what happens after we die. They say that knowing that we have only one life makes us value it even more.

Most Christians and Muslims believe that we have two lives: this one and the next ever-lasting one. If we have been good in this life, after we die, we get our bodies back and go to heaven and live with God forever. But if we have been bad, we are sent to hell to be tortured forever. The process of getting our bodies back is called **resurrection**.

Indian religions like Buddhism, Jainism, Sikhism and Hinduism say that we have many lives. We continue to be reborn in new bodies. This is called **reincarnation** or **the cycle of rebirth**. We only escape from the cycle of rebirth when we realise our real nature as one with God.

If we have lived before, why don't we remember our past lives?
Hinduism says it is because we actually do not want to remember our past lives. If we remember who we were in our past lives, we may become very sad as it will remind us of all the family and friends we have left behind. So we actually do not want to remember our past lives. It is perhaps better that way. But there have been cases where some children suddenly remember their past lives and tell others about it. The details they give of a past life can sometimes be checked to see if they are true. In many cases these details match the facts.

Something continues to live after our bodies stop working

In some cases, when patients are undergoing operations in hospitals, they seem to have died for a short while. Their lungs, hearts and even their brains stop working. After some time, these patients wake up and recount what happened to them after the body seemed to have died. They recall unusual experiences of after-life. Such experiences are called **Near Death Experiences**. Such cases make us believe that something continues to live, even after the body has died.

The importance of religions in dealing with death

We all feel scared when we think about dying. We do not want to leave all our friends and family and our favourite things behind. When we die, all these things will be snatched away from us. Religious teachings can help us deal with death. They give us comfort and hope that our souls continue to live. Reincarnation teaches that we may even meet up with our loved ones in another life.

Reincarnation is a fairer system

Reincarnation offers us comfort that if we did not get a chance to achieve certain things in this life, we will get another chance in our next life or lives. It also teaches us that we must develop a good character, because this is the only thing that stays with us and comes with us when we die. That is why, right from the time they are born, children in the same family exhibit such varied characters. They have developed their characters over many previous lives. A person who is kind and caring will be reborn as kind and caring. A person who has worked hard to develop certain skills like music or art, will be reborn with natural talents in these fields.

What about animals?

Hinduism agrees with the theory of evolution that says that we are the continuation of the animal kingdom. Hence we must treat animals with care. They are not so different from human beings. Hinduism does not agree that animals were put on earth for human consumption. Hinduism teaches that all of us started off as simple life forms and then evolved into human beings over millions of years. Once we have evolved out of the animal kingdom, we must give up violence and aggression. We must be kind and caring and treat everyone and everything with respect. Animals bred for human consumption are often treated very cruelly; that alone should be a good enough reason to become **vegetarian**.

Story of Shambhu and the mad king

There was once an ancient kingdom ruled by a mad king. The mad king had a habit of inviting people to his palace and then killing them. Everyone feared being invited to the palace. One day, the king's messenger brought the invitation to a simple man called Shambhu. Shambhu was very frightened. He knew that he would be killed by the mad king. What could he do? Shambhu ran quickly to his best friend's house to ask him for help. The friend felt very sad. He said, 'Shambhu, you are my very dear friend. I will come with you up to the palace gates but I will not come inside the palace with you.' Shambhu felt very sad, he was relying on his best friend to help him out. As he was walking home he met an acquaintance who asked him why he was looking so sad. Shambhu told him the story. The acquaintance said, 'Do not worry. Not only will I come with you, I will go ahead of you and plead on your behalf.' Shambhu was amazed. Who was this person and why was he helping him so much?

So what is this story all about? The mad king is the king of death. One by one, he invites all of us to visit him. We are all frightened of dying, and become scared. At the time of death, we turn to those we love most: our family and friends. They support us and help us, but they cannot come with us when we die, they can only accompany us to the grave. Then who is this acquaintance who pleads on our behalf? The acquaintance, who we hardly think about, is the character we have built for ourselves. It is our character that accompanies us when we die and makes us what we are in our next life.

The only thing that accompanies us when we die is the character we have developed. Hence we should pay a great deal of attention towards building up a good character as that is the only thing that comes with us when we are re-born.

Being born again and again, is it really that good?

Getting another chance

It is nice to think that we will get another chance to do things we did not get an opportunity to do in this life. We can start from where we left off in the previous life. Suppose someone has an ambition to become a great musician, but then unexpectedly he dies. Reincarnation will make sure that when that person is reborn, he will be born with natural talent for music.

Getting a new body

As we get older, our bodies become wrinkled and diseased. We become forgetful. We are no longer able to hear or see clearly. Reincarnation ensures that we get fresh bodies to carry on with what we want to do.

Having to go to school again and again

But there is a downside to reincarnation. It means that we have to live in mummy's tummy again. We have to become a baby again, and re-learn how to walk and talk. And we have to go to school again! Though, the next time round, we may be more clever, though we may not remember why.

It might become a bit boring

After being born so many times, we may begin to feel a bit bored at having to go round and round. We then look for a way out. The only way out is to find out who we truly are. We are Atman, a spark of God. Once we find this out we do not care to be born again. We then become one with God and gain **moksha**.

Learning about Religion

❖ Three views about life after death:
   - Humanists and Atheists say that there is only one life
   - Christians and Muslims say that we have two lives
   - Hindus, Buddhists, Jains and Sikhs say that we have many lives
❖ Samsar is the cycle of rebirth
❖ Moksha brings the cycle of rebirth to an end by uniting us with God
❖ Yoga means joining with God or discovering our real Self as God
❖ NDE: Near Death Experiences suggest that something carries on living even when the body has died for a short time

Learning from Religion

❖ How do ideas of life after death affect the way we lead our lives?
❖ How can the way we live our lives make any difference to what happens to us after we die?
❖ What do we think happens to us between births?
❖ When we dream, where does the dream world come from?
❖ Are heaven and hell created by our minds between lives?
❖ What do we like doing most? Does it reflect what we did in our past life?
❖ What skills do we think we have brought from our previous lives?

Classroom Activities

❖ Write a story about who you may have been in your previous life
❖ Discuss: The Mystery of Life:
   (1) Investigate what Science says about how life began?
   Compare this with views from Hinduism and Christianity
   (2) Why is life so precious? Compare what science says with what religions say?
❖ From our website download, enlarge and print:
   (a) A poster showing the cycle of life and death
   (b) The game: *Moksha*

Chapter 8
My Family

Living in a family

Being brought up in a loving family is a wonderful experience cherished by all children. Family life teaches us how to live with each other in a caring way. Living in a family gives us a sense of belonging, and also gives us a unique identity. Children are taught to respect their parents and to care for the elderly members of the family. Grandparents help look after the grand children in a caring and loving manner.

This is how everyone in the family gets support and love from each other. The Hindu religion promotes the idea of extended families. An extended family includes parents, children and grandparents living together. Sometimes extended families include uncles and aunts and cousins. In some cases they may live close to each other for support. Hinduism promotes the idea that grandparents must be cared for by the family and should not be sent off to old-people's homes.

We must live for others

Hinduism teaches that we should not only learn how to live *with* each other, but learn to live *for* each other. This means that we must not be selfish. It is good to start a family with a loving partner. The pair can then set up home to bring up their children and look after their parents. The idea of looking after others must be extended to taking care of all the people in the community and society. Living for others is the best way of putting religion into practice.

Story of Krishna and Sudama

When Krishna was a young boy, his best friend was called Sudama. They both lived with their teacher. One day, the teacher asked Krishna and Sudama to go to the forest and bring back some firewood. The two little boys went into the forest, but then, suddenly the sky darkened. A thunderstorm arrived. The boys quickly climbed up a tree and sat on one of the branches. They were cold, wet, and hungry. Sudama suddenly remembered that he had been carrying a bag of puffed rice. He was feeling very hungry, and there was not much to share, so he did not tell Krishna about the puffed rice. When Krishna was not looking, Sudama quietly ate up all the puffed rice. Krishna is God, so he knew everything, but kept quiet. The next morning, the storm passed, and the boys returned to their teacher. Many years passed by. Krishna and Sudama finished school and went their separate ways. Krishna became a king, but Sudama could not find any work. He became poorer and poorer. He lived in a tiny hut with his family.

Sudama decided to visit Krishna to ask for help. But then he thought: 'How can I visit my friend without taking a present for him?' His wife told him, 'We have some puffed rice, why don't you take that as a present for Krishna?' 'What a silly thing to offer a king!' thought Sudama. But there was nothing else to offer, so he took the puffed rice with him. When Sudama reached Krishna's palace, Krishna came running out to see him. He was so happy to see his old friend. Krishna noticed the bag of puffed rice Sudama was carrying and asked, 'What have you brought for me?' Sudama felt ashamed of his silly gift and was trying to hide it. But Krishna would not let him hide the bag. He quickly pulled it out and with delight, started to eat the puffed rice. While Krishna was eating the puffed rice, something magical started to happen. Sudama's hut began to turn into a palace. Sudama had been suffering because he had been mean in his childhood. The moment he offered God what he had, his condition improved.

This story says that we must not be mean; we must share what we have with others. When we help others, we are serving God, because it is God who lives in everyone. When we serve others, our condition improves.

Hindu values

❖ **Why be truthful?** Because by being truthful we feel nicer and closer to God. When we lie, we feel uneasy; we cheat ourselves and others.

❖ **Why be peaceful and non-violent?** Because that makes us feel closer to all living things. Hurting others makes us feel isolated and distant from everyone.

❖ **Why be celibate?** Hinduism teaches that young people should be celibate, specially when they are studying. Otherwise their minds are distracted and they cannot focus on their studies.

❖ **Why be kind and loving to others?** Hinduism teaches that it is God alone who appears as everything and everyone.

❖ **Why should we treat everyone equally?** Everyone is a spark of God and should be given equal dignity and respect. Respect should also be extended to the animal and plant kingdoms. The environment should also be treated with respect and not be exploited needlessly.

No one is higher or lower than anyone else

In every society, there are always some people who group themselves together and consider themselves to be better or higher than others. They turn their noses up at others who they see as beneath them. They treat other people as unequal, and do not give them equal opportunity. Pre-judging others with wrong or limited understanding is called **prejudice**. This may result in mistreating others which is called **discrimination**.

❖ **Class prejudice**: The English Class system is one example of class prejudice. The Caste system in India is another example.

❖ **Racial prejudice**: Having wrong notions about someone due to the colour of their skin is called racial prejudice.

❖ **Gender prejudice**: Having wrong notions about someone just because they are of different gender is called gender prejudice.

Religious teachings oppose all prejudices and the discrimination that may occur due to such prejudices.

The Holy Cow

The Hindus do not worship the cow but respect it. The reason why they respect the cow is because they view this animal as man's best friend. Cows have been giving milk to mankind for thousands of years without asking for anything in return. It is a friendly and gentle animal that deserves special reverence. That is why Hindus call the cow, *holy*. Hindus show respect for all other animals by linking them with Gods and Goddesses.

Hereditary caste system is unjust

No one should be classed as being impure, or belonging to a lower class. Many Hindu leaders have tried to get rid of such hurtful divisions in Hindu society. One example is that of Ghanshyam Maharaj, the head of the **Swaminarayan** movement. One day, he deliberately went to the house of a very poor man who was considered to be impure and from the lowest class. Ghanshyam Maharaj told him, 'I am very hungry. Give me some food.' The poor man was very surprised, he always thought that he was from a lower class, hence his food was impure and not fit for a religious leader. The poor man felt very pleased, and happily offered his simple food to Ghanshyam Maharaj, who ate it happily.

This is how Hindu leaders teach the importance of giving equal dignity to all human beings.

Learning about Religion

* Living in an extended family allows one to practise how to live for each other
* Extend the idea of who we call our family to take on more and more people
* Hinduism teaches equality and justice for everyone because everyone is a reflection of God
* We must extend the idea of reverence for life to include the animal kingdom
* Prejudice means pre-judging or misjudging others
* Discrimination means treating others as unequal

Learning from Religion

* How can big families make us feel comfortable and give us a sense of identity and belonging? What are the draw-backs?
* The role of the family in promoting religious beliefs and practices in daily life
* Think about religious and non-religious responses to:
  Why do we feel nice when we see others happy?
  Why do we feel sad when we see others in distress?
* Can we extend the idea of our family to incorporate our neighbours? What would be the difficulties?
* Why do we feel nice when we think well of others and feel terrible if we think badly of others for any length of time?

Classroom Activities

* Write an essay on why we should treat everyone as equal, even though we know that everyone is actually quite different from everyone else
* Discuss: How prejudices can be hidden. How in most cases, we may not even be aware that we have prejudices?
* Examine our own prejudices
* Do we really think that girls are equal to boys?
* What do we think of new migrants who come to this country?

Chapter 9
Thinking about others

Helping the poor

Hinduism teaches that we must look after our families and members of our community and society. God is in us as well as in everyone, so helping others is the same as helping ourselves. We must not ignore the poor people of the world. We have to do our best to help them in every way.

Some things are not fair

Children born in rich families in rich countries have lots of things to eat, many toys to play with, and many clothes to wear. Many children born in poor countries do not have enough food to eat, or enough clothes to wear. Many of these poor people do not even have clean water to drink. Many of these children do not get an opportunity to go to school to become educated. Often they are made to go to work even though they are just children. Some things are not fair.

Going to a party

Imagine two boys going to a party where they are given a lovely chocolate cake to share. Suppose one of the boys is a big bully and decides to eat the chocolate cake all by himself, and only gives crumbs to the other boy. Will that be fair? The big bully will scoff down the whole chocolate cake and feel sick, while the other boy will go home feeling hungry. We must not allow this to happen, but this is already happening in the world today. Some of the richer countries act like big bullies. They buy goods and services from the poorer countries without paying them a fair price.

Religion teaches us to share what we have with others. It tells us not to be greedy or bully people who are less fortunate than us.

Too much or too little!

Children in rich countries are offered so many things to eat, that they eat too much and become obese and unhealthy, while many children in poor countries become ill and die, because they do not have enough to eat. This is very strange; children in rich countries become ill because they have too much to eat while children in poor countries die because they do not have enough to eat. Even though there is enough food in the world so that everyone can be well fed, some are eating too much and wasting too much, while others are not getting enough. This is not right. We have to act more responsibly and devise a fairer system.

How can we help?

We have to help people in poor countries. We can help them by giving them food, clothes and medicine. Better still, we can help them become educated. This will help them earn a living for themselves. Then they do not have to rely on the charity of others. This is the best way of helping the poor. This allows them to earn a living, and live with dignity.

We have to become aware of the unfair system of world trade

Richer nations are able to buy goods and services from the poorer nations at give-away prices because they are strong and can dictate the terms of business. Ordinary men and women in rich nations have to be made aware of these unfair trade practices. They should only buy goods and services that have been bought at a fair price. In this way, a fairer system of trade will benefit the people in poor countries. They deserve to be paid a fair price for the goods and services they sell.

Why should we look after others?

People who belong to Monotheist religions (those who believe in a God) believe that as we are created by the same God, we must help others because they too have been created by the same God. If we do so, God will be pleased with us and reward us. If we hurt or harm other human beings, God will be displeased with us and will punish us. This sounds like a good reason for being moral, but then there are people who do not believe in God. They say that we must look after each other because that is the best way we can live in harmony with each other. They say that we can help others without believing in God or religion.

Poverty on the other side of the world

We cannot call ourselves truly religious or civilised if we do not do something to remove the dire poverty in some parts of the world. Hinduism teaches: 'Vasudeva Kutumbakam', which means: 'The whole of mankind belongs to the same family.' Hence, when any members of the family are in need, others family members must come to their aid.

Just because we help others, should we feel proud?

It is not good to feel proud or show off when we help others. The same God who lives in us also lives in everyone else. So when we help others, we are actually helping ourselves. Helping ourselves cannot be called charity! It is the least we can do for ourselves.

Naren, the boy who liked to give everything away

In India lived a little boy called Naren. Whenever he saw any poor people, he became very sad and wanted to do something for them. But what can a little boy do? Every time a beggar knocked on his door asking for money, little Naren would pick up the best thing he could find in his house and give it away.

His father noticed that one by one, everything from his living room was disappearing. He decided to keep a watch. One day, he caught little Naren giving something away to a beggar. He asked Naren, 'What are you doing?' Naren replied, 'Father, they have nothing, so we must give them something.' Naren's father was secretly pleased to see that his son was so compassionate. But he did not like losing all the valuable things from his living room!

So from that day on, whenever there were beggars at the door, Naren was locked up in his mum's bedroom. Naren felt annoyed, because he wanted to do something for the poor people who came to their door. What could he do? He noticed his mum's wardrobe and opened it. In the cupboard he saw stacks of colourful, expensive saris. It looked like treasure to the little boy. He quickly opened the bedroom window and called out to the beggars, 'Come to the window! I have something to give you'. Soon the little boy was handing out all his mum's expensive saris to the poor people, who were quite surprised. They blessed the little boy for being so caring.

Of course, when Naren's parents found out what was happening, they quickly stopped him. They pretended to be very angry, but in their hearts, they knew that the boy was doing the right thing. When the boy grew up, he became famous as Swami Vivekananda.

He taught the people of the world that the best way to worship God is by serving the poor people of the world.

Learning about Religion

❖ Recognise that there is a serious divide between the rich and poor and, that enough is not being done to address this issue
❖ The need to help those who are less well off than ourselves
❖ We must help others because we are all made by the same God and God will be pleased with us for helping others
❖ Should we help others if we do not believe in God or religion?
❖ Hinduism teaches that when helping others, we are actually helping ourselves. This is the correct attitude to adopt when doing charitable work

Learning from Religion

❖ How can religious teachings be helpful in tackling poverty?
❖ Why is compassion so important? Does compassion require belief in religion?
❖ How did Vivekananda inspire people to help the poor?
❖ List the reasons why many people continue to ignore the issue of poverty?
❖ To what extent are we fulfilling our duties to the third world?
❖ What do people mean by human rights, and why are they so important?
❖ How can human rights be compromised by poverty?

Classroom Activities

❖ Choose a local charity the school can support
❖ Raise funds through weekly cake sales etc
❖ Sponsor sports activities like walks to raise funds
❖ Discuss the statement by Gandhi:
  There are enough resources for man's needs but not enough for man's greed
❖ Investigate how the third world debt arose and why it should be written off.

Practical Ideas

Practising fair trade in the classroom
Ask your school to buy fair trade food and drinks. Fair trade goods are bought from poor countries by paying a fair price for the goods. So the poor people receive a good price for the goods they sell us.

Try to set up a fair trade event in your school, telling people in the rest of the school what fair trade is, and by setting up a stall selling fair trade chocolate, biscuits and fruit juices.

You can also ask your parents to start buying fair trade food and drinks like tea and coffee from supermarkets.

The Shoebox Appeal
Arrange for your class to take part in a 'shoe-box appeal', where every one goes home and fills a shoe-box with toys, sweets, and a letter, and wrap the box with colourful paper and ribbons to send as a gift to a child in the third world.

Holding Charity Events
Organise an event like a play, music or fashion show in order to collect funds for a chosen charity or school in a third world country. Write letters and stay in touch with the children at this school, and see how the funds are being used.

Chapter 10
Unity in diversity

Religious pluralism

Hindus are allowed to think of God in different ways. People of other religions think of God in even more different ways. Hinduism teaches that all religions lead to the same God. There are as many ways of thinking about God as there are people. As we are all very unique, the way we think about and relate to God will also be very unique and special. This is called religious pluralism.

Many rivers merging in the same ocean

Imagine lots of rivers flowing down the mountainside. Some may be huge, some may be small. Some may flow in a straight line, some may meander a lot. Some may be noisy, some may be silent. They all originate in different parts of the mountain and yet end up and merge in the same ocean. In the same manner different religions originated in different parts of the world; some religions may have huge number of followers, some may have a handful of followers. Some may be loud, some may be very quiet, yet all these religions lead us to the same God (spirit). Asking someone to change their religion is like asking a river to go up the mountain and come down another way. It is foolish. That is why Hindus dislike the idea of persuading people to change their religion. We must never force our ideas of religion on other people. We must appreciate that everyone is making spiritual progress in their own unique way.

Is any one religion better than others?

Hinduism does not agree that any one religion is better than any other. When any one religion makes such claims, it creates bad feelings between people of different religions. It can result in fighting in the name of religion. Pluralism teaches that the religion that suits our own needs is the best for us. That is why we must not force it on people of other religions. They have different needs which are fulfilled by their religion. We must not go to people of other religions and bully them into changing their religion.

Different religions are different ways of looking at the same God

Think of a house. One person sees it from the front. He says that it has four windows and a front door. But someone else may see the same house from the back. He would describe the back porch and the garden. Someone viewing the house from the side will see something completely different. The same house is described differently, by different viewers. The same is true of different religions. They reflect different approaches in making spiritual progress.

Many ways of discovering spirituality

Hinduism teaches that the essence of the universe, and ourselves, is something quite different from matter. It is called Brahman~ spirit. Becoming spiritual means discovering that we are essentially the spirit, and not just a complicated lump of matter. Some of us become spiritual using religions. Some of us become spiritual using other means.

Spirituality at the heart of other human disciplines

The reason why some of us are attracted to music, or art or dance or literature or poetry or even science, is because all of these disciplines remind us about the spiritual nature of the whole universe, including ourselves. That is why Hinduism accepts that all these disciplines can make us spiritual without reference to God or religion.

The story of Ramakrishna

About a hundred years ago in India, lived a man called Ramakrishna. Ever since he was a little boy, he was able to experience God. If he saw something beautiful in nature, he would feel a thrill. He would feel connected with the whole universe. He could experience that it was God who had become everything. Seeing that everything is actually God, or Brahman, is one of the most exciting ways of experiencing God.

When Ramakrishna was a young boy, he helped his brother who was a priest in a temple of the Mother Goddess. Ramakrishna wondered: 'Can anyone actually see the Mother Goddess in real life?' Just seeing the statue of the Mother Goddess was not enough for him. He wanted to see the real Mother Goddess. He prayed very hard. Sometimes he would pray for the whole night without going to sleep. He kept praying to the Mother Goddess every day and every night for many years, crying: 'Oh Mother, if you are real, then show yourself to me.' One day, when he wept bitterly, he suddenly saw, with open eyes, the whole world disappearing! Everything, including the temple and the ground he was standing on, disappeared. He saw huge waves of light coming towards him from all directions, and then he saw the Mother Goddess smiling and blessing him.

From that day on, he was able to see the Mother Goddess whenever he wished. She would talk to him, play with him, and give him advice. This is the true story of a person who was able to see God and talk to God like a real person.

Ramakrishna then wanted to experience God through other religions. He spent time learning about and practising Christianity and Islam. In a very short time, he was able to experience God as described in these religions. This is the first time a person was able to experience God using so many different ways. He was able to see God as the Mother Goddess, he was able to experience God as his inner self: Atman. He was able to see God as everything: Brahman. He was able to experience God using the Christian and Muslim ways. He has proved that all religions lead to the same God.

He taught: We must not fight over which religion is best. Even though all religions look very different, they all lead to the same God.

God has many names

There was a lake that provided good drinking water. On one side of this lake lived some Hindus. They used to draw and drink water from their side of the lake. The word for water in their language was *jal*. On another side of the lake, lived some Muslims. They also drank water from the same lake. The word they used for water was *pani*. At another part of the lake, Christians drank the same water. And, of course, they called the water, *water*. One day, all these people met up and started arguing about the name of the nutritious drink they all lived on and where to get it from. They all had different names for it, and used different pathways to reach it. They started arguing and fighting about what it is called, and how to reach it.

A wise man who was passing by, asked them why they were arguing. The wise man knew the many sides of the lake, and he also knew the many names for water in different languages. He told them, 'You are arguing for no reason. The nutritious drink you are all talking about is the same thing. You are using different pathways to reach the same lake and drink the same thing, even though you call it by different names. There is no reason to fight. Use your own pathways to reach the water, drink it and be happy rather than fight over it.'

Hindus say that God is addressed differently by different religions. Different religions promote different ways to find God. Rather than fight and argue with people of other religions, we should use the methods prescribed by our religion to think about and reach God.

Inter-faith dialogue

Interfaith dialogue is the name given to the discussion between people of different religions. The Hindu religion offers something unique to this dialogue. It affirms that other religions are true. It teaches that we must not use words like 'tolerate' in inter-faith dialogue, because that suggests that other religions are somehow inferior. Pluralism accepts that there are many ways of thinking about and finding God. Other religions should not only be tolerated, they should be recognised and accepted as valid pathways for making spiritual progress.

Hinduism and Science

Hinduism agrees with the findings of modern science. It claims that modern science reveals the spiritual foundation of the universe.

The Theory of Evolution

Hinduism agrees with the theory of evolution. It agrees that we are a continuation of the animal kingdom. This should make us take greater care of all the animals.

What is life?

Life is considered very special and precious. This is not so because some bits of matter accidentally got wound up in a unique manner and became alive; but because something very special called the spirit made itself visible in the material universe.

The Theory of Big-Bang

Hinduism agrees with the theory of Big-Bang. This theory says that the universe was created billions of years ago with the unfolding of time and space. It teaches that when the cycle of creation is over, the universe will fold up with a big crunch. Hindus call each cycle of creation and destruction a **Kalpa**.

The Origin of Life

Biologists say that life first appeared on earth as a single-celled being about four billion years ago. Human beings emerged, through a process of evolution over billions of years. The Hindu religion agrees with all this, but disagrees that the process of evolution is accidental; it claims that this process is directed.

Links between Hinduism and findings of Modern sciences are explored in greater detail in our publication *Hinduism for Schools.*

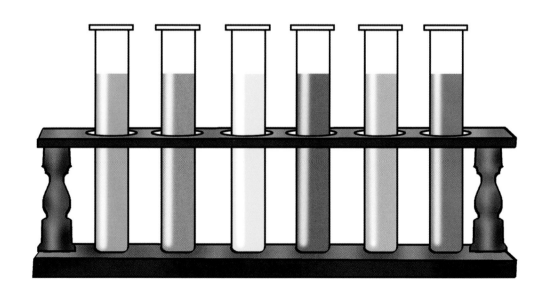

Hinduism and the Arts

Hinduism makes use of art, music, dance, drama, literature, and poetry to explore and express religious ideas. Religions are very subtle. All forms of art specialise in giving expression to subtle things. That is why all art forms are excellent tools to express or explain religious ideas.

Art

Temple architecture, beautifully carved images, or colourful rangoli patterns, are some of the different ways Hindus use art to express religious ideas. Grand temple designs with elaborate carvings on its pillars; intricate patterns used in mandala patterns and the brightly coloured rangoli patterns are some of the ways art is used to invoke ideas about spirituality.

Literature

Literature and Poetry are wonderful tools for expressing religious ideas. Hinduism has lots of colourful stories in the Epics and the Puranas to explain many subtle ideas in their religion. Upanishads that express Hindu philosophy are presented in a poetic form. Poetry has the power to express things which are difficult to express in prose.

Dance and drama

Stories of the Ramayana and Mahabharata are performed as dramas in which players act out different roles. These dramas are performed during festivals and other ceremonies. Sometimes these dramas are set to music and performed as dance dramas.

Role of music

Music can focus our minds in a unique manner and allow us to get a glimpse of our spiritual nature. Hinduism encourages the use of music to make us feel spiritual. The Sama Veda, one of the Vedas, is set to music.

Can a person be spiritual without believing in God or religion?

Hinduism agrees that a person can be spiritual without believing in God or without being religious. There are many people who do not believe in God, but are wonderful human beings. Hinduism says that such people have discovered how to be spiritual without using religion. Some of us become spiritual using religion and some of us prefer to do so without using religion. Everyone is in fact already spiritual, because the essence of every living being is the spirit ~ Atman.

Role of Hinduism in modern times

Hinduism has a great deal to contribute towards reconciling the truth claims of different religions. Without this reconciliation, we face the danger of conflict between people of different religions. Promoting religious pluralism is the best way of resolving this serious issue.

Reconciling the truth claims between a science oriented world-view with a religiously oriented world-view is another area where Hinduism can make a very positive contribution. Hindus view spirituality to be the common subject matter of modern sciences as well as religion. It is not only the prophets of the past, but the science of today that has the power to draw mankind to spirituality.

Learning about Religion

❖ Pluralism: there can be many ways of thinking about God (or spirituality), and many ways of relating to God (or spirituality).

❖ Spirituality can be expressed in a non-religious mode, through arts, music, poetry and science.

❖ Brahman: God as the spiritual underpinning to everything and everyone; becomes more visible as living things; becomes most clearly visible as men and women.

❖ Ramakrishna: experienced the same God using Christianity, Islam and a range of pathways promoted in Hinduism (God as the Mother Goddess, God as Atman and God as Brahman).

Learning from Religion

❖ Does inter faith dialogue mean people of different religions *just* talking to each other? Suggest what else they can do.

❖ Discuss the challenges and opportunities for a multi-faith society.

❖ What are the similarities and differences between teachings of different faiths?

❖ Can there be a variation of views within a single religion?

❖ Examine what all religions say about people of *other* religions.

❖ What are the names of God in different religions? Are these names significant?

❖ Are there religions without a God? What do they have instead of God?

❖ Many Humanists do not believe in God. They just want to live a good life. Does this mean that they will be punished by God?

❖ Can science ever find God?

❖ How can art, music or dance make us feel spiritual?

❖ Explore the limitation of language in expressing spirituality.

❖ What is the role of poetry in religion?

Classroom Activities

❖ Visit our website and use links to Hindu sites to view and hear creative and expressive Hindu art, music, and Sanskrit recitations. How do they manage to convey spirituality?

❖ Make a pie chart of the number of students who believe in God, the number who are not sure about God and the number who are quite sure there is no God.

❖ Discuss: The best way to be spiritual is to believe in God.

Resources

Hinduism for Schools website: www.hinduism.fsnet.co.uk

This is the main website that offers access to activities suggested at the end of each chapter of this book. It also offers various links for ICT projects.

For teachers' guide notes:

email hindu@btinternet.com

To Buy *Primary Hinduism* or *Hinduism for Schools* textbooks:

Contact Seeta Lakhani

6 Lea Gardens, Wembley Middlesex, HA9 7SE

Tel: (++44-20) 8902 0840 Email: hindu@btinternet.com

Vivekananda Centre London

Website with links to the Ramakrishna order

and literature related to Vedanta and Swami Vivekananda

www.vivekananda.co.uk

For arranging a visit to a Hindu temple:

Shri Swaminarayan Mandir (BAPS)

105-119 Brentfield Road, Neasden, London NW10 8LD, UK

Tel: (++44-20)8965 2651 Fax: (++44-20)8965 6313

Email: admin@mandir.org

For other books on Hinduism:

Hindu Sahitya Kendra

46-48 Loughborough Road, Leicester LE4 5LD, UK

Tel: (++44) 0116 261 1931 Fax: (++44) 0116 261 1931

Email: info@hskonline.co.uk

Other Hindu resources:

Himalayan Academy

Kauai's Hindu Monastery, 107 Kaholalelel Road, Kapaa, Hawaii USA

Tel: 967646 9304 Fax (1) 808-822-4351 Phone (1) 800-890-1008

Website: www.himalayanacademy.com

Arranging a visit to a Hindu Monastery or to obtain books on Vedanta:

Ramakrishna Vedanta Centre Blind Lane, Bourne End,

Buckinghamshire SL8 5LG Tel: (++44) 016285 26464

Website: www.vedantauk.com Email: vedantauk@talk21.com

Glossary

Arati	A ceremony to welcome God
Ahimsa	The value of not hurting or harming anyone or anything
Atman	God as your true self
Avatar	Name given to Vishnu when He comes to earth to help mankind
Brahma	God as the creator of the universe
Brahman	God appearing as everything
Caste System	The division of society; but is often misused as an excuse for prejudice
Darshan	To see an image of God in a holy place
Deity	A form of God
Dharma	Noble living; the name given to Hinduism
Diwali	Festival of Lights
Durga	Parvati in the form of the destroyer of evil
Dushera	The tenth day of the festival of the Mother Goddess
Fasting	The act of avoiding certain foods on holy days
Ganesh	The elephant-headed God who brings good luck
Ganges	One of the most sacred rivers in India
Gita	One of the most important holy books of Hinduism
Guru	A spiritual teacher
Hanuman	The monkey-headed deity of strength
Hindu	The mispronounced name of the river 'Sindhu'
Holi	The festival of spring and colour
Karma	Action; 'The Law of Karma' says that everything we do has a result
Krishna	An 'avatar' (see above) of Vishnu; teaches us how to find God in different ways
Lakshmi	The goddess of wealth and beauty

Lotus	The flower of purity and detachment
Mahabharata	The longest epic of Hinduism about Krishna and the Pandava brothers
Moksha	The end of the cycle of rebirth; finding God
Murti	An image of God
Namaste	Hindu greeting: 'I bow down to God as you'
Navaratri	The festival of nine nights; worshipping the mother goddess
Om	Sound heard in the deepest of meditation
Parvati	The mother goddess; 'Shakti' or power
Prashad	Food that has been offered to God
Pratik	A symbol of God
Pratima	An image of God
Puja	Worship of God in the home or temple
Puranas	Legends and fun stories of Hinduism
Rama	An 'avatar' (see above) of Vishnu; the ideal man
Ramakrishna	A recent prophet of Hinduism; experienced God through Christianity, Islam and Hinduism
Ramayana	An epic of Hinduism; the story of Rama, Sita and Hanuman
Reincarnation	A belief that the soul is born again and again
Rishi	A person who can see God and tell us about God
Samsara	Reincarnation; the cycle of rebirth
Sanskrit	An ancient Indian language
Saraswati	The goddess of learning, art, and music
Shakti	Energy or power of the Mother Goddess
Shiva	One of the forms of God in Hinduism
Sita	The wife of Rama
Swami	A holy man or monk

Swastika	A symbol of good luck
Tilak	A mark on the forehead; identifies a person as Hindu
Vedas	Knowledge of God that comes from someone who has seen God
Vishnu	God in the form of the preserver of the universe; comes to earth in the form of 'avatars'
Vivekananda	A recent proponent of Hinduism; emphasises the divinity of mankind
Yoga	The act of joining with God

Index